Contents

Ant bodies

Hurry! Ants rush by.

They carry food.

Ants are busy!

Ants have three main body parts.
They have six legs.

head

thorax

abdomen

Some ants are red or yellow.

Other ants are black or brown.

9

Ant homes

Ants may make nests
under ground or
inside tree trunks.
Some make big mounds.

11

Lots of ants live

in each nest.

They work together.

13

Work, work

Most ants are workers.

They find food.

Workers carry food
to the nest.
They feed the young.

17

Baby ants

The queen ant lays tiny eggs.

A worm-like larva grows

in each egg. It wiggles out.

The larva makes a soft shell around itself. Inside, it turns into an ant. Hello, ant!

Glossary

larva insect at a stage between an egg and an adult

mound hill or pile; ants may make nests in tall mounds on the ground

nest home of an animal

queen female ant that lays eggs

worker adult female ant that does not lay eggs; worker ants build nests, find food and take care of young ants

Read more

Ants (Creepy Crawlies), Rebecca Rissman (Raintree, 2013)

Let's Look for Minibeasts: A Natural History Activity Book, Caz Buckingham and Andrea Pinnington (Fine Feather Press, 2015)

Minibeast Body Parts (Comparing Minibeasts), Charlotte Guillain (Raintree, 2012)

Websites

www.bbc.co.uk/cbeebies/shows/mini-beast-adventure-with-jess
Go on a minibeast adventure with Jess, and discover the minibeasts that are on your doorstep!

www.woodlandtrust.org.uk/naturedetectives/activities/2015/06/minibeast-mansion/
Design and build your own minibeast mansion!

Comprehension questions

1. Where do ants make nests? Give two examples.
2. Name two of the jobs that worker ants do.

Index

body parts 6

eggs 18

food 4, 14, 16

larvae 18, 20

legs 6

mounds 10

nests 10, 12, 16

queen ants 18

workers 14

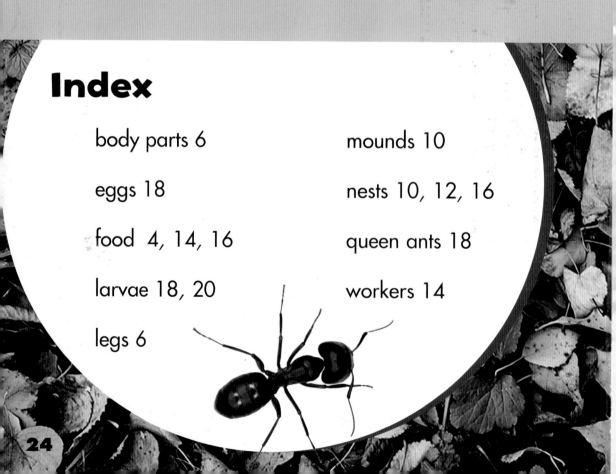